WORLD OF WORK

STEM

Exploring Career Pathways

Diane Lindsey Reeves

Created and produced by
Bright Futures Press, Cary, North Carolina
www.brightfuturespress.com

Published by
Cherry Lake Publishing, Ann Arbor, Michigan
www.cherrylakepublishing.com

Photo Credits: Cover, Beautyline; page 7, 8, 3DDock; page 7, 10, SUWIT NGAOKAEW; page 7, 12, goodluz; page 7, 14, Creativa Images; page 7, 16, angellodeco; page 7, 18, Sorin Colac; page 7, 20, jannoon028; page 7, 22, saiko3p; page 24, omelchenko.

Library of Congress Cataloging-in-Publication Data

Names: Reeves, Diane Lindsey, 1959- author.
Title: STEM / Diane Lindsey Reeves.
Description: Ann Arbor, Michigan : Cherry Lake Publishing, [2017] I Series:
  World of work I Audience: Grades 4 to 6. I Includes bibliographical
  references and index.
Identifiers: LCCN 2016042184I ISBN 9781634726283 (hardcover) I ISBN
  9781634726481 (pbk.) I ISBN 9781634726382 (pdf) I ISBN 9781634726580
  (ebook)
Subjects: LCSH: Science--Vocational guidance--Juvenile literature. I
  Technology--Vocational guidance--Juvenile literature.
Classification: LCC Q147 .R385 2017 I DDC 502.3--dc23
LC record available at https://lccn.loc.gov/2016042184

Printed in the United States of America.

TABLE OF CONTENTS

Hello, World of Work..4

Take a Hike..6

WoW Up Close..7

    Automotive Engineer..8

    Chemist..10

    Environmental Engineer..12

    Epidemiologist..14

    Geneticist..16

    Naval Architect..18

    Statistician..20

    Zoologist..22

WoW Big List..24

Take Your Pick..26

Explore Some More..27

My WoW..30

Glossary..31

Index..32

HELLO WORLD OF WORK

This is you.

Right now, your job is to go to school and learn all you can.

This is the world of work.

It's where people earn a living, find purpose in their lives, and make the world a better place.

Sooner or later, you'll have to find your way from **HERE** to **THERE**.

To get started, take all the jobs in the incredibly enormous world of work and organize them into an imaginary pile. It's a big pile, isn't it? It would be pretty tricky to find the perfect job for you among so many options.

No worries!

Some very smart career experts have made it easier to figure out. They sorted jobs and industries into groups by the types of skills and products they share. These groups are called career clusters. They provide pathways that will make it easier for you to find career options that match your interests.

- Architecture & Construction
- Arts & Communications
- Business & Administration
- Education & Training
- Finance
- Food & Natural Resources
- Government
- Health Sciences
- Hospitality & Tourism
- Human Services
- Information Technology
- Law & Public Safety
- Manufacturing
- Marketing
- Science, Technology, Engineering & Mathematics (STEM)
- Transportation

Good thing you are still a kid.

You have lots of time to explore ideas and imagine yourself doing all kinds of amazing things. The **World of Work** (WoW for short) series of books will help you get started.

TAKE A HIKE!

There are 16 career pathways waiting for you to explore. The only question is: Which one should you explore first?

Is **Science, Technology, Engineering,** and **Mathematics (STEM)** a good path for you to start exploring career ideas? There is a lot to like about careers in this pathway. Developing cutting-edge medicine and products. Engineering solutions for transportation, construction, manufacturing, and so many industries. Creating innovative new technologies and finding new ways to use data, statistics, and other valuable information.

See if any of the following questions grab your interest.

WOULD YOU ENJOY concocting experiments in a science lab, trying out the latest smartphone, or taking advanced math classes?

CAN YOU IMAGINE someday working in a science laboratory, engineering firm, or research and development center?

ARE YOU CURIOUS ABOUT what aeronautical engineers, ecologists, statisticians, oceanographers, or zoologists do?

If so, it's time to take a hike! Keep reading to see what kinds of opportunities you can discover along the STEM pathway.

But wait!

What if you don't think you'll like this pathway?

You have two choices.

You could keep reading, to find out more than you already know. You might be surprised to learn how many amazing careers you'll find along this path.

OR

Turn to page 27 to get ideas about other WoW pathways.

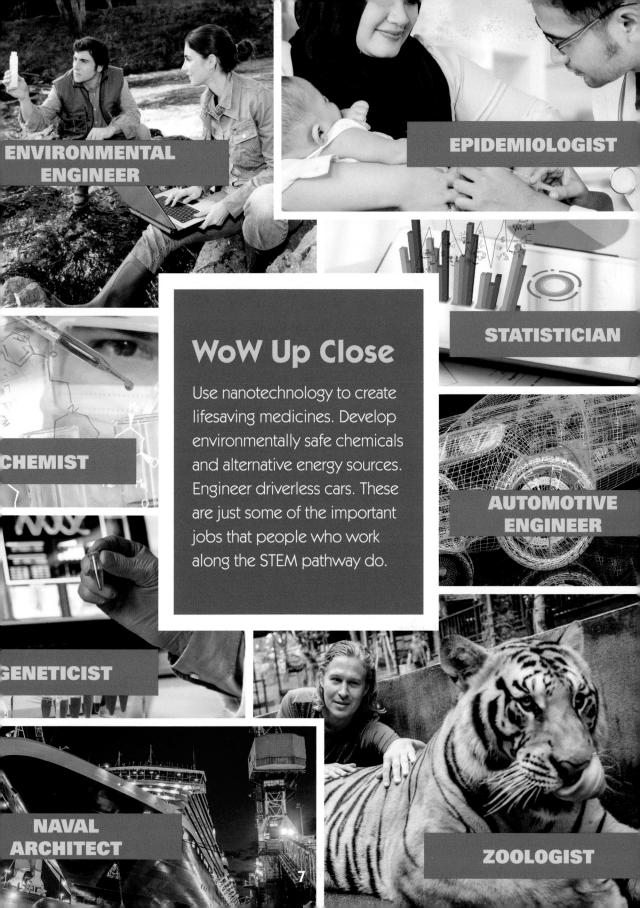

ENVIRONMENTAL ENGINEER

EPIDEMIOLOGIST

STATISTICIAN

WoW Up Close

Use nanotechnology to create lifesaving medicines. Develop environmentally safe chemicals and alternative energy sources. Engineer driverless cars. These are just some of the important jobs that people who work along the STEM pathway do.

CHEMIST

AUTOMOTIVE ENGINEER

GENETICIST

NAVAL ARCHITECT

ZOOLOGIST

AUTOMOTIVE ENGINEER

Cars. Trucks. Buses. Motorcycles. Recreational vehicles. **Automotive engineers** design and improve the vehicles that keep people on the go.

The vehicles we use every day have come a long way since Henry Ford's **assembly line** made it possible for people to replace horses and buggies with cars. Automotive engineers still design new models of vehicles every year. They still find solutions to engineering problems through research and development. And they still help manufacturers figure out the best way to produce vehicles.

But today's automotive engineers are also working on exciting new challenges. Think driverless cars. Think **hybrids** and other eco-friendly cars. They are also rethinking new types of mass transit. They are even developing vehicles that robots can drive on Mars!

The road to becoming an automotive engineer often starts by taking auto shop classes in high school. It also helps to take lots of high-level math classes. Then it's off to college to earn a degree in mechanical or automotive engineering. After a couple of years of experience and lots of studying, it will be time to take a test that makes it official. That's when you become a licensed professional engineer.

Check It Out!

Go online to find out how cars are made at

- http://bit.ly/MakeaCar
- http://bit.ly/AssemLine
- http://bit.ly/ElectCar

Start Now!

- ✔ Make your own "soap box car." Use the Internet to find do-it-yourself instructions.

- ✔ Pay attention to the different makes and models of cars you see on the road. Download pictures of the ones you like best on the Internet and compare the different features.

- ✔ Use the Internet and library resources to construct a timeline on the "history of transportation."

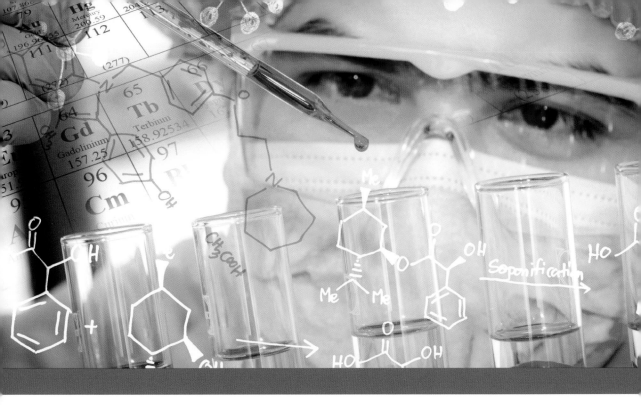

CHEMIST

Chemicals are everywhere. They are in our bodies and in the food we eat. They are in the clothes we wear and all over the houses we live in. You'll find them in the medicine cabinet, in your mom's makeup bag, and in your family's cleaning supplies. Your school backpack is full of them, too.

In fact, the American Chemical Society keeps track of more than 120 million different chemical substances in its gigantic database. **Chemists** are scientists who research and experiment with these different chemical substances to create products we use every day. And they are creating new chemical substances every day.

Chemists work in pretty much any industry you can imagine. They work in laboratories and use powerful computers and other tools to do their work. Since there are so many different chemical substances, chemists tend to specialize in certain kinds. Biochemists work only with those chemicals and reactions that occur in living organisms. These chemists develop lifesaving medicines. Forensic chemists use chemistry to investigate evidence and crack crimes.

All chemists took lots of science and math classes in high school. They also went on to study chemistry in college.

Check It Out!

Find kid-friendly adventures in chemistry at

- http://bit.ly/AdvenInChem
- http://www.chem4kids.com

Start Now!

- ✔ Use the Internet and library resources to find ideas for "chemistry experiments for kids."

- ✔ Create a chart or poster showing the chemicals that are found in the human body.

- ✔ Make a list of the different chemicals you find at home in cleaning and grooming products.

ENVIRONMENTAL ENGINEER

Environmental engineers care about the environment. They use engineering skill and scientific know-how to solve problems with recycling, waste disposal, and safe water and air supplies. Their number one goal is to take good care of Planet Earth.

Sometimes they work to correct problems that have already happened. This might be air pollution caused by a factory or water pollution caused by an oil spill. Other times they work to prevent problems from happening in the first place. This is especially true of the earth's natural resources like oil and wood, air and water. Environmental engineers look for alternative energy sources using solar power and wind. They develop new ways to reduce how much water people use.

Finding better ways for people and the environment to get along is a big part of what environmental engineers do. Whether it is setting up recycling programs, turning waste into electrical power, or finding new ways to reduce air and water pollution, their work makes the world a better place.

It's all about finding **sustainable** ways of doing things that don't use up natural resources.

Check It Out!

Find out more about issues that environmental engineers care about at

▶ https://toxtown.nlm.nih.gov

▶ http://www.eia.gov/kids

▶ http://bit.ly/WaterEPA

▶ http://bit.ly/KidsAir

Start Now!

✔ See what ideas you can come up with to improve your family's recycling efforts.

✔ Make a list of ways you can reduce the use of water and electricity at home and at school.

EPIDEMIOLOGIST

Epidemiologists are disease detectives. They look at how and why disease outbreaks start. Then they figure out how diseases are spread among people so they can treat the disease and keep it from causing more harm.

If certain diseases go unchecked, they can cause an epidemic. Epidemics are caused by diseases that spread so quickly that a lot of people get sick at one time or in one place. Every winter, medical doctors warn people to get their flu shots to prevent a flu epidemic.

Sometimes epidemiologists must go out into the "field" to track down the source of an outbreak. They interview people, collect water and food samples, and conduct other kinds of tests. Other times an epidemiologist uses computers to study a disease. Things like **statistics** and **big data** help them better understand what is going on.

It takes a lot of training to become an epidemiologist. Most epidemiologists have earned at least a master's degree in public health. This training prepares them to work in health departments for state and local governments, in hospitals, and at colleges and universities. Some work for organizations like the World Health Organization and track down diseases all over the world.

Check It Out!

Find links to several videos about infectious diseases at

▶ http://www. diseasedetectives.org/ videos

Then play some germy games at

▶ http://www. diseasedetectives.org/ microbe_dance

Start Now!

Go online to track down infectious diseases and solve medical mysteries before it's too late at

✔ http://medmyst.rice.edu

✔ http://www.mclph.umn. edu/watersedge

✔ http://www. epidemicgame.org/index. html

GENETICIST

Are your eyes brown, green, or blue? Do you have light hair or dark? Is your hair curly or straight? Do you look more like your mother or your father? The answers to these questions can be traced to your **genes**. Genes are one of the parts that make up the **chromosomes** that make up you.

Genes are passed from parents to children. The genes you inherit determine what you look like and the way you will grow.

Genes do more than give you your looks. While some diseases are caused by germs, others are passed down through the genes. These are called genetic disorders, and they include **Down syndrome**, **sickle-cell anemia**, and even some forms of **cancer**.

Some **geneticists** are doctors who specialize in medical problems that can be inherited through a person's genes. Geneticists study a person's genetic makeup through saliva and blood tests and other medical procedures. Results from these tests help them evaluate, diagnose, and manage patients who have **hereditary** diseases.

Other geneticists are scientists who conduct research to discover new medicines and better ways to detect genetic diseases. Genetic researchers are unlocking many mysteries and making important scientific breakthroughs all the time.

Check It Out!

Explore genetics online at

- https://www.genome.gov/genomiccareers
- http://bit.ly/MyMonsterDNA

Start Now!

- ✓ Make a family gene tree showing the traits that you (and any siblings) inherited from each of your parents.

- ✓ What is DNA, and what does it have to do with your genes? Use the Internet and library resources to find out.

NAVAL ARCHITECT

Naval architects and marine engineers design, build, and repair all kinds of ships. This includes military aircraft carriers and submarines, tankers, cargo ships, and other vessels used in industry. It also includes luxury cruise ships and sailboats.

No matter what the vessel is used for, naval architects design ships that look good and perform well in the water. Stable hulls are a must. After all, who wants to create a ship that sinks?

Naval architects use some of the same types of tools as an architect who designs buildings. They use special computer programs to make models and test concepts. They create very specific and extremely complicated blueprints that are used to construct the vessel. They also work with teams of engineers and other experts to make sure that every detail is carefully considered.

Designing seaworthy vessels is very different from designing vehicles for dry land. Naval architects first get a college degree in mechanical or electrical engineering. Then they get special training from one of the maritime academies, which prepare students for sea-related professions.

Check It Out!

See what you can find out about these famous ships:

- Niña, Pinta, and Santa Maria
- RMS Titanic
- USS Arizona

Start Now!

- Use the Internet and library resources to find out how to build your own "ship in a bottle."

- Make a chart to compare and contrast the differences and similarities of a cruise ship used to take passengers on exotic vacations and battleships used by the military.

- Sketch out your ideas for a ship of the future.

STATISTICIAN

These professionals conduct polls to predict who will win presidential elections. They gather data on every move athletes make during professional sports events. They make forecasts about what the weather will be like tomorrow and next week. They figure out where hospitals and schools are needed.

Who are they? They are **statisticians**. Statisticians use numbers to find answers for real-world problems. They reach logical conclusions by gathering large amounts of data and **analyzing** it very carefully.

If you are thinking that statisticians must be math whizzes, you are correct. They are also scientists. Statistics is the science of learning from data. Put these two skills together and you get information that shapes everything from elections and the environment to the stock market and sports.

Here's an example of how it works. Let's say a statistician is hired to conduct a poll of potential voters in an election. He or she can use a poll to find out who voters plan to vote for and why. When voters read the results in media reports, they can be influenced in both positive and negative ways. That's why it is so important to get the numbers right.

Check It Out!

Add up new information about statistics at

➤ http://bit.ly/SportsStat

➤ http://bit.ly/WhatStat

➤ http://bit.ly/WhyStat

Start Now!

✔ Make a chart to keep track of the sports statistics of a favorite sports team or athlete.

✔ Find all kinds of probability and statistics activities at http://bit.ly/ProbStatAct.

✔ Read more about what statistics is all about at http://thisisstatistics.org.

ZOOLOGIST

You probably know that some **zoologists** take care of animals at zoos. They make sure animals are fed the right foods, get plenty of exercise, and are given the right medicines to stay healthy. But did you know that zoologists work to create **natural habitats** for zoo animals? They also work hard to protect **endangered species**.

Zoologists are animal experts. They get so well acquainted with certain species of animals that they understand how these animals live, think, and behave. They use all this knowledge in different ways. The care and feeding of animals is one way. Figuring out how to mimic life on a savannah or rain forest in the middle of a big U.S. city is another way. It is amazing how creative zoologists get when building a home away from home for different kinds of animals.

Other zoologists research ways to save different types of animals from extinction. This can involve anything from working on reproduction issues to retraining animals to live in the wild.

Lots of people love animals and would like to work with them—especially in zoos. The people who land zoo jobs are well trained and have lots of experience with animals.

Check It Out!

Get acquainted with successful zoologists at

- http://bit.ly/ZooCare
- http://bit.ly/ZooAfrica
- http://bit.ly/ZooLife

Start Now!

- See what some of your favorite animals are up to at the San Diego Zoo: http://kids.sandiegozoo.org/animal-cams-videos.

- Make a poster showing care and feeding instructions for your favorite zoo animal.

- Visit online zoos at http://www.theonlinezoo.com and http://www.waza.org/en/zoo.

Accountant • Actuary • Aerospace engineer • Agricultural engineer • Anthropologist • Archaeologist • Architectural drafter • Archivist • Astronomer • Atmospheric and space scientist • **AUTOMOTIVE ENGINEER** • Biochemical engineer • Biochemist • Bioinformatics technician • Biomedical engineer • Biophysicist • Biostatistician • Cartographer • Chemical technician • **CHEMIST** • Civil engineer • Clinical research coordinator • College professor • Computer-aided design and drafting (CADD) specialist • Computer hardware engineer • Computer scientist • Computer systems analyst • Conservation

WoW Big List

Take a look at some of the different kinds of jobs people do in the STEM pathway. **WoW!**

Some of these job titles will be familiar to you. Others will be so unfamiliar that you will scratch your head and say "huh?"

scientist • Cost estimator • Curator • Database administrator • Dietetic technician • Economist • Educator • Electrical engineer • Electromechanical technician • Electronic engineering technician • **ENVIRONMENTAL ENGINEER** • **EPIDEMIOLOGIST** • Ergonomist • Financial advisor • Financial analyst • Fire prevention engineer • Food scientist • Fuel cell engineer • **GENETICIST** • Geodetic surveyor

• Geographer • Geological engineer • Geological technician •
Geoscientist • Health and safety engineer • Human factors engineer
• Hydrologist • Industrial ecologist • Industrial health and safety
engineer • Industrial psychologist • Logistician • Logistics engineer
• Manufacturing engineer • Mapping technician • Marine architect
• Marine engineer • Materials engineer • Materials scientist •
Mathematician • Mechanical engineer • Mechatronics engineer •
Medical scientist • Microbiologist • Mining safety engineer •
Nanosystems engineer • Natural resources manager • Natural science

Find a job title that makes you curious. Type the name of the job into your
favorite Internet search engine and find out more about the people who
have that job.

1 What do they do?

2 Where do they work?

3 How much training do they need to do this job?

manager • **NAVAL ARCHITECT** • Nuclear technician • Nutritionist •
Oceanographer • Park naturalist • Petroleum engineer • Pharmacologist
• Photogrammetrist • Physicist • Political scientist • Product safety
engineer • Quality control analyst • Sociologist • Software developer
• Solar energy system engineer • **STATISTICIAN** • Survey researcher
• Teacher • Technical writer • Wildlife biologist • **ZOOLOGIST**

TAKE YOUR PICK

	Put stars next to your 3 favorite career ideas	Put an X next to the career idea you like the least	Put a question mark next to the career idea you want to learn more about
Automotive engineer			
Chemist			
Environmental engineer			
Epidemiologist			
Geneticist			
Naval architect			
Statistician			
Zoologist			
	What do you like most about these careers?	What is it about this career that doesn't appeal to you?	What do you want to learn about this career? Where can you find answers?

Which Big Wow List ideas are you curious about?

Please do **NOT** write in this book if it doesn't belong to you. You can download a copy of this activity online at www.cherrylakepublishing.com/activities.

EXPLORE SOME MORE

The STEM pathway is only one of 16 career pathways that hold exciting options for your future. Take a look at the other 15 to figure out where to start exploring next.

Architecture and Construction

WOULD YOU ENJOY making things with LEGOs™, building a treehouse or birdhouse, or designing the world's best skate park?

CAN YOU IMAGINE someday working at a construction site, a design firm, or a building company?

ARE YOU CURIOUS ABOUT what civil engineers, demolition technicians, heavy-equipment operators, landscape architects, or urban planners do?

Arts & Communications

WOULD YOU ENJOY drawing your own cartoons, using your smartphone to make a movie, or writing articles for the student newspaper?

CAN YOU IMAGINE someday working at a Hollywood movie studio, a publishing company, or a television news station?

ARE YOU CURIOUS ABOUT what actors, bloggers, graphic designers, museum curators, or writers do?

Business & Administration

WOULD YOU ENJOY playing Monopoly, being the boss of your favorite club or team, or starting your own business?

CAN YOU IMAGINE someday working at a big corporate headquarters, government agency, or international business center?

ARE YOU CURIOUS ABOUT what brand managers, chief executive officers, e-commerce analysts, entrepreneurs, or purchasing agents do?

Education & Training

WOULD YOU ENJOY babysitting, teaching your grandparents how to use a computer, or running a summer camp for neighbor kids in your backyard?

CAN YOU IMAGINE someday working at a college counseling center, corporate training center, or school?

ARE YOU CURIOUS ABOUT what animal trainers, coaches, college professors, guidance counselors, or principals do?

Finance

WOULD YOU ENJOY earning and saving money, being the class treasurer, or playing the stock market game?

CAN YOU IMAGINE someday working at an accounting firm, bank, or Wall Street stock exchange?

ARE YOU CURIOUS ABOUT what accountants, bankers, fraud investigators, property managers, or stockbrokers do?

 ## Food & Natural Resources

WOULD YOU ENJOY exploring nature, growing your own garden, or setting up a recycling center at your school?

CAN YOU IMAGINE someday working at a national park, raising crops in a city farm, or studying food in a laboratory?

ARE YOU CURIOUS ABOUT what landscape architects, chefs, food scientists, environmental engineers, or forest rangers do?

 ## Government

WOULD YOU ENJOY reading about U.S. presidents, running for student council, or helping a favorite candidate win an election?

CAN YOU IMAGINE someday working at a chamber of commerce, government agency, or law firm?

ARE YOU CURIOUS about what mayors, customs agents, federal special agents, intelligence analysts, or politicians do?

 ## Health Sciences

WOULD YOU ENJOY nursing a sick pet back to health, dissecting animals in a science lab, or helping the school coach run a sports clinic?

CAN YOU IMAGINE someday working at a dental office, hospital, or veterinary clinic?

ARE YOU CURIOUS ABOUT what art therapists, doctors, dentists, pharmacists, and veterinarians do?

 ## Hospitality & Tourism

WOULD YOU ENJOY traveling, sightseeing, or meeting people from other countries?

CAN YOU IMAGINE someday working at a convention center, resort, or travel agency?

ARE YOU CURIOUS ABOUT what convention planners, golf pros, tour guides, resort managers, or wedding planners do?

 ## Human Services

WOULD YOU ENJOY showing a new kid around your school, organizing a neighborhood food drive, or being a peer mediator?

CAN YOU IMAGINE someday working at an elder care center, fitness center, or mental health center?

ARE YOU CURIOUS ABOUT what elder care center directors, hairstylists, personal trainers, psychologists, or religious leaders do?

Information Technology

WOULD YOU ENJOY creating your own video game, setting up a Web site, or building your own computer?

CAN YOU IMAGINE someday working at an information technology start-up company, software design firm, or research and development laboratory?

ARE YOU CURIOUS ABOUT what artificial intelligence scientists, big data analysts, computer forensic investigators, software engineers, or video game designers do?

Law & Public Safety

WOULD YOU ENJOY working on the school safety patrol, participating in a mock court trial at school, or coming up with a fire escape plan for your home?

CAN YOU IMAGINE someday working at a cyber security company, fire station, police department, or prison?

ARE YOU CURIOUS ABOUT what animal control officers, coroners, detectives, firefighters, or park rangers do?

Manufacturing

WOULD YOU ENJOY figuring out how things are made, competing in a robot-building contest, or putting model airplanes together?

CAN YOU IMAGINE someday working at a high-tech manufacturing plant, engineering firm, or global logistics company?

ARE YOU CURIOUS ABOUT what chemical engineers, industrial designers, supply chain managers, robotics technologists, or welders do?

Marketing

WOULD YOU ENJOY keeping up with the latest fashion trends, picking favorite TV commercials during Super Bowl games, or making posters for a favorite school club?

CAN YOU IMAGINE someday working at an advertising agency, corporate marketing department, or retail store?

ARE YOU CURIOUS ABOUT what creative directors, market researchers, media buyers, retail store managers, and social media consultants do?

Transportation

WOULD YOU ENJOY taking pilot or sailing lessons, watching a NASA rocket launch, or helping out in the school carpool lane?

CAN YOU IMAGINE someday working at an airport, mass transit system, or shipping port?

ARE YOU CURIOUS ABOUT what air traffic controllers, flight attendants, logistics planners, surveyors, and traffic engineers do?

MY WoW

I am here.

Name _____

Grade _____

School _____

Who I am.

Make a word collage! Use 5 adjectives to form a picture that describes who you are.

Where I'm going.

The next career pathway I want to explore is

_____

Some things I need to learn first to succeed.

1 _____

2 _____

3 _____

My Career Choice

To get here.

GLOSSARY

analyzing examining something carefully in order to understand it

assembly line an arrangement of machines and workers in a factory, in which a product passes from one person or machine to the next, with each performing a small, separate task, until it is completely assembled

automotive engineer person who designs and manufacturers automobiles and other vehicles

big data extremely large amounts of information that are analyzed by computers to reveal patterns, trends, and associations

cancer a serious disease in which some cells in a body grow faster than normal cells and destroy healthy organs and tissues

chemist person who conducts research using chemical substances for the purpose of creating new products and medicines

chromosomes the structures inside the nucleus of a cell that carry the genes that give living things their individual characteristics

Down syndrome a genetic disorder in which a person is born with learning disabilities and with eyes that appear to slant, a broad skull, and shorter fingers than normal

endangered species a plant or animal that is in danger of becoming extinct

engineering all the jobs involved in the work of designing and creating large structures (such as roads and bridges) or new products or systems by using scientific methods

environmental engineer person who uses engineering skills and scientific know-how to solve problems about recycling, waste disposal, and safe water and air supplies

epidemiologist person who studies the causes, distribution, and control of disease in populations

genes one of the parts that make up a chromosome that are passed from parents to children and determine how you look and the way you grow

geneticist biologist who is an expert about genes, heredity, and variations of organisms

hereditary the process of passing physical and mental qualities from a parent to a child before the child is born

hybrids cars with a gasoline engine and an electric motor, each of which can propel them

mathematics all the jobs involved in using mathematical methods in science, engineering, business, computer science, and industry

natural habitat the place in nature that particular species calls home

naval architect person who designs, builds, and maintains ships and other types of marine vessels and structures

science all the jobs involved in planning, managing, and providing scientific research and professional and technical services, including laboratory and testing services and research and development services

sickle-cell anemia a genetic blood disease in which many normal red blood cells take on a sickle shape and cannot carry oxygen

statistician math expert who uses huge amounts of data to figure out how likely it is that something will happen

statistics facts or pieces of information taken from a study that covers a much larger quantity of information

sustainable done in a way that can be continued and that doesn't use up natural resources

technology all the jobs involved in using science and engineering to do practical things, such as make businesses and factories more efficient

zoologist person who is an expert about animals

INDEX

Adventures in Chemistry, 11*

AirNow, 13*

American Chemical Society, 11

American Statistical Association, 21*

Architecture & Construction, 5, 27

Arizona State University, 17*

Arts & Communication, 4, 27

assembly line, 9

Business & Administration 5, 27

cancer, 17

Chem4Kids, 11*

Chicago Revealed, 23*

chromosomes, 16

Disease Detectives, 15*

Down syndrome, 17

Education.com, 21*

Education & Training, 5, 27

Energy Kids, 13*

Environmental Protection Agency, 13*

Epidemic, 15*

ESPN, 21*

European Auto Source, 9*

Extra Minutes, 23*

Finance, 5, 28

Food & Natural Resources, 5, 28

Ford, Henry, 9

Government, 4, 28

Health Sciences, 5, 28

Hospitality & Tourism, 5, 28

Human Services, 5, 28

Information Technology, 5, 29

Law & Public Safety, 5, 29

Lincoln Park Zoo, 23*

Manufacturing, 5, 29

Marketing, 5, 29

Mars, 9

MedMyst, 15*

National Human Genome Research Institute, 17*

Niña, 19

Online Zoo, 23*

Outbreak at Watersedge, 15*

Pinta, 19

Rice Center for Technology in Teaching and Learning, 15*

Ruiz, Camila, 23*

San Diego Zoo, 23*

Santa Maria, 19

Science, Technology, Engineering & Mathematics, 5Scott, Jonathan 23*

sickle-cell anemia, 17

This Is Statistics, 21*

Titanic, RMS, 19

ToxTown, 13*

Transportation, 5, 29

University of Minnesota, 15*

U.S. Census Bureau, 21*

U.S. Energy Information Administration, 13*

U.S. National Library of Medicine, 13*

USS Arizona, 19

WaterSense Kids, 13*

World Association of Zoos and Aquariums, 23*

World Health Organization, 15

YouCar, 9*

* Refers to the Web page sources

About the Author

Diane Lindsey Reeves is the author of lots of children's books. She has written several original PEANUTS stories (published by Regnery Kids and Sourcebooks). She is especially curious about what people do and likes to write books that get kids thinking about all the cool things they can be when they grow up. She lives in Cary, North Carolina, and her favorite thing to do is play with her grandkids—Conrad, Evan, Reid, and Hollis Grace.